T0361252

Routledge Revivals

Poverty in Plenty

First published in 1931, this *Routledge Revivals* title reissues J.A Hobson's analysis of financial distribution in the early years of Twentieth Century Britain. The book focuses on the moral questions that he considered to be important in regard to the economic reforms that were necessary to secure the utilisation of modern productivity for the welfare of mankind. In this work, Hobson considers the wasteful working of the economic system, with its over-production, under-consumption and unemployment and states that these errors are due to the unfair way in which income is apportioned among the nations, classes and individuals that produce it. *Poverty in Plenty* argues for a conscious economic government inspired by a sense of justice and humanity. It makes suggestions towards the establishment of such a government and presents business prosperity as a problem of morals.

Poverty in Plenty

The Ethics of Income

J. A. Hobson

Routledge
Taylor & Francis Group

First published in 1931
by George Allen & Unwin Ltd

This edition first published in 2012 by Routledge
2 Park Square, Milton Park, Abingdon, Oxon, OX14 4RN

Simultaneously published in the USA and Canada
by Routledge
711 Third Avenue, New York, NY 10017

Routledge is an imprint of the Taylor & Francis Group, an informa business

Publisher's Note
The publisher has gone to great lengths to ensure the quality of this reprint but
points out that some imperfections in the original copies may be apparent.

Disclaimer
The publisher has made every effort to trace copyright holders and welcomes
correspondence from those they have been unable to contact.

ISBN 13: 978-0-415-62328-5 (hbk)
ISBN 13: 978-0-203-10252-7 (ebk)

POVERTY IN PLENTY

THE ETHICS OF INCOME

by

J. A. HOBSON

LONDON
GEORGE ALLEN & UNWIN LTD
MUSEUM STREET

FIRST PUBLISHED IN 1931

PRINTED IN GREAT BRITAIN BY
UNWIN BROTHERS LTD., WOKING

PREFACE

All business men and economists admit that there are grave defects in the present working of our economic system. But they differ widely in their diagnosis. Many regard the present trouble as only a larger, more intense and widespread example of those trade depressions which recur periodically, natural and necessary fluctuations in the tide of industry. Important war and post-war disturbances in production, markets, finance, have made this depression worse and more wasteful than others—that is all. Others, however, find a unique economic character in this depression. Some trace this uniqueness to the rapid pace and unpredictable direction of recent advances in the technique of power-driven machinery and the organisation of production and markets, displacing obsolete methods and 'economising' labour. Unemployment they regard as an inevitable cost of economic progress. Others find the uniqueness in an insufficiency and a maldistribution of gold and of purchasing power which by its effect on prices has crippled the activity of business men and loaded industry with increased indebtedness to the 'rentier' class.

That these causes aggravate the situation it is not my intention to deny. But the prominence afforded to them helps to screen the great fundamental source of trouble, the lack of any conscious equitable government of industry. While the closest application of conscious planning to the operations of each single business is everywhere recognised as essential to success, the extension of this process to the economic system as a whole has got no purchase on the business mind. Yet the adjustments between trade and trade in the national and world markets are as delicate as those between the departments in a single business and demand as much conscious care.

This refusal to apply reason to the conduct of the wider business life is closely related to the moral purblindness that accompanies all economic activities. Moralists have often exposed the selfish pursuit of personal gain as a degrading motive in the business life, but they have not shown its paralysing influence upon the production and enjoyment of wealth.

In this little book I seek to demonstrate how the determination of prices by economic force for personal gain operates through inequitable distribution of income and property to cause maladjustment in production and consumption with attendant unemployment, poverty, and waste. The blunting of moral perception and sensibility by the habitual acceptance of untrue notions about business operations is the chief obstacle to the reforms needed to secure the utilisation of modern productivity for the welfare of mankind. It is the moral basis of this reformation that I wish to lay in these chapters. With a brief indication of the desirable lines of reconstruction, I leave policy to those whom it concerns.

J. A. HOBSON

HAMPSTEAD

June 1931

CONTENTS

POVERTY IN PLENTY

CHAPTER I

THE LACK OF ECONOMIC GOVERNMENT

Until now most business men, industrialists, mer-
chants, financiers, who looked outside the particular
operations in which they were engaged, have believed
in the existence of an economic system towards which
their activities contributed and which, with some
allowances for waste and friction, was reasonable,
equitable, and efficient. Though there existed no
direct and conscious unitary control, or government,
of this economic system, certain laws of supply and
demand, expressing the play of competitive self-
interest among buyers and sellers of goods and
services, were believed to lead everyone, capitalist,
worker, or landowner, to apply his productive power
in ways most serviceable to society as a whole.

The plight in which the world finds itself to-day has
destroyed this conception of an economic system
with the complacency it engendered. I am not here
concerned with Marxist or other schools of socialists,
but with ordinary business men averse from rapid
revolutionary changes, who are staggered in their
minds by the failure of the system which they have
always believed to work with ordinary efficiency.
They were accustomed formerly to periodic depressions with a wastage that was relatively small, partial,

passing, and believed to be essential to economic progress.[1] The depression they see to-day is deeper, longer, wider, and blocks production in nearly all industries and all countries. An earlier disposition to regard this economic trouble as a by-product of the Great War no longer suffices as an explanation. For the ravages war made in the human and material resources of many countries, the collapse of monetary systems, the diversion of trade routes, the erection of high tariffs, and other forms of economic nationalism, should have shown some disposition to yield to 'time the healer.' Moreover, all these injuries must express themselves in a reduced productivity of the economic system, whereas the actual trouble that confronts us is the existence in almost all industries and all countries of a producing power that is excessive, in the sense that a large part of it—land, capital, and labour—stands idle because the goods it could produce cannot find a market at prices covering the bare costs of production.

Now this is a new situation in the history of capitalism, so dangerous that it has shattered the general belief in the existence of a rational economic system. The 'invisible hand,' which compelled men in serving themselves best to serve the public best, is quite evidently inoperative. For the first time there has arisen, outside the range of visionaries and utopians, among the ranks of plain practical men a

[1] "Our modern system of industry will not work without some unemployed margin, some reserve of labour" (Charles Booth, *Life and Labour*, Vol. I, p. 152).

widely voiced demand for conscious planning in the business world so as to rescue it from anarchy.

Everywhere among thoughtful men the issue is that of economic government or anarchy. Though statesmen may try to shed their responsibility by treating the situation as a natural phenomenon, advising us to 'wait for the turn of the tide,' or 'for the sun to break through the clouds,' reasonable men and women in growing numbers hold that trade, industry, and finance are branches of human conduct, individual and collective, and that man's reasonable will should and can regulate this conduct. In other words, while natural phenomena, such as drought and pestilence, may and do affect the productivity of certain countries, they are of diminishing importance, owing to closer world communications and improved storage, and can shed no light upon the current situation with its excessive productivity. Quite evidently it is not nature but man that is to blame for the welter of unsaleable goods and the waste of unused capital and labour that attest the collapse of our 'economic system.'

The demand for rational order has first taken shape in a new attitude towards combines, cartels, and other trade organisations. Formerly it was only the business unit that was subject to a rational economy, each part or process being adjusted to the needs and utility of the business as a whole. Now this 'rationalisation' is being extended to national or even international industries as organic wholes. But the order or economy which such rationalisation seeks

to establish is not conceived or applied in the equitable interest of society as a whole, but for the more
profitable exploitation of a particular industry in the
interests of the owners of its share capital. The
elimination of the waste of competition between the
business units which form a cartel or other combination for the profitable working of a particular
industry does not normally accrue to the advantage
of the consumer, though the employees of this
rationalised industry may sometimes share in
higher wages the advantages of a price-fixing
economy.

This partial application of the process of rationalisation is, however, perhaps the best approach
towards a study of the several problems involved in
a rational government of industry. For it affords an
insight into the nature of the existing misrule.

We may tabulate the fundamental defects of this
industrial misrule as follows, beginning with the
narrower settings.

1. There exists no equitable criterion for the rates
of pay, wages, or salaries, for manual or mental
workers in the various processes of production of
goods or services in this or any other country.
Neither risk to life or health, physical or mental
effort, skill, initiative or responsibility, utility or
other quality of product, determines pay or other
conditions of employment to any appreciable extent
in most occupations. Again, needs or standard of
living, except so far as supported by a strong
organisation with bargaining power, do not regulate

payment on any intelligible scale beyond the bare subsistence rate. Neither from the side of cost of production nor of utility of consumption does our economic system work with equity, rationality, or economy. As between one class or grade of workers and another, wage-rates and salaries are determined by strength of 'pull.' A skilled farm labourer gets less than a dustman, a builder's labourer, or a postman; employees in the textile and metal trades, exposed to the full brunt of foreign competition, are worse paid than most grades of railwaymen or routine workers in the printing trades. Strength of organisation, shelter from foreign or other distant competition, command of markets in key industries—these conditions, severally or jointly, are the main direct determinants of wage-rates. A 'strong' trade union can force up wages, often paid not out of surplus profits but out of higher prices paid by other workers, i.e. by reducing the real wages of their 'comrades.' In a word, the term 'fair wages' has no ascertained meaning, and, if it had, the present 'system' affords no means of ensuring such a payment.

2. While the material capital (plant, raw material, etc.), managerial and technical ability in their various grades are essential co-factors in a business, the owners of the share capital are the sole legal owners of that business, which is operated with a single object of making dividends for them. If a business prospers, the whole measure of its prosperity usually goes in profits to the owners, though the activities of brain and hand of the employees, together with the

favourable conditions of the market, are manifestly the operative causes of the prosperity. Nor is it a fair reply to say that the owners also bear the losses in reduced value of their capital and lower dividends. For when a business ceases to pay, or makes a loss, though capital suffers, labour usually suffers more, either from wage-cuts which hurt the worker and his family more than loss of dividends the capitalist and his family, or from unemployment or short time, which mean destitution qualified by the 'dole.'

In other words, the sole ownership of a business by the owners of its share capital denotes an inequitable structure. For in reason and morals it equally belongs to the owners of the other active factors of production, the brain and hand workers who contribute to its product and depend for their livelihood upon its regular efficient working. There is a cleavage between the legal and the 'real' ownership that finds damaging expression in a constant bickering and occasional conflict between the capital and labour whose harmonious co-operation is essential to full efficiency. No reasonable rules for the pacific settlement of such conflicts exist, or for the apportionment of the income of a business between the several factors of production. Terms like 'fair wages' and 'reasonable rate of profit' have no clear ascertainable meaning, and there exists no criterion of a 'just price' for a Consumers' Council to apply.

3. Recent large and rapid fluctuations in monetary values, or price-levels, have disclosed another source

of unreason, injustice, and waste in the working of the economic system, by emphasising the conflict of interest between the passive and the active factors of industry. In the wild inflation of the war and post-war periods large masses of fixed interest payments in the shape of mortgages, debentures, pensions were cancelled or greatly reduced in many countries to the advantage of ordinary shareholders, and an era of 'profiteering' upon a hitherto unknown scale ensued. Some classes of wage-earners shared to a less extent in the gain from this cancelment of fixed charges upon industry.

Since the resumption of the gold standard in this and certain other countries, a reversal of this earlier unreason and inequity has been achieved through a deflationary fall of prices, which has greatly increased the burdens of war-indebtedness and of all other fixed charges, securing to the owners of such charges an increased share of the real income of the nation. This injury to the ordinary capitalist quite evidently cripples business enterprise, and no remedy is provided under the current working of our economic system.

4. The apportionment of the national income and of the general income of the world between the stronger and the weaker industries in the several countries is based upon no sound principles of justice or economy. Economic force is the agent of distribution. Within each nation a certain number of sheltered or protected trades, often internally combined, with powers to restrict output and fix selling

prices, and handling goods or services that are of vital and indispensable importance to the community, are in a position to levy tribute upon other trades and the consuming public, taking a share of the national income which measures their economic strength, not their skill, efforts, or needs.

This seizure of an unearned surplus by organised economic force has, of course, a wider sphere of action than the nation. It is a marked and disconcerting feature of the world-economy. Almost everywhere the growers of foods and raw materials, widespread and ill-organised, are at the mercy of banks or local money-lenders, the owners of transport and storage, and the wholesale dealers who handle their product and often finance its production. This weakness of the farmer in most countries is a source of growing discontent. Many agricultural products are handled by wholesale agents and by retail local traders so as to apportion a small and diminishing proportion of the final retail price to the farmer.

There are other important cleavages of interest in the realms of industry and finance, sometimes within the national area, sometimes in the world markets. Wherever effective combination displaces or limits competition, in the national or international markets, that efficiency of combination means a higher price, usually achieved by an agreed restriction either of output or of market, or both. In an increasing number of commodities, many of them highly specialised articles, such as chemicals and the rarer metals, international cartels are in control, regulating prices and raising costs of production in the various industries to which these articles are indispensable. Within Great Britain, during the years of this deep general depression, tobacco, drink, and a few other luxury trades have taken an increasing toll of the reduced real income of the nation.

Our 'economic system' does not pretend to furnish any remedy for these grave injustices or to place the claims of the different trades to their share of the general income upon any equitable basis.

5. Finally, we encounter the wastes and injustices involved in the economic application of the principle of national sovereignty, the claim that each nation is the absolute owner and controller of all the economic resources, natural and human, within its domains. This economic nationalism assumes two shapes in modern times. The first is the attempt by trade regulations to conserve the economic resources of the country for the exclusive advantage of the existing inhabitants thereof, by restricting the entry of foreign competing goods and labour, or by the limitation of exports. Protective tariffs and immigration restriction are chief instruments of this economic nationalism. But the need of advanced industrial nations for large and secure access to backward countries with weaker populations, in order to obtain upon favourable terms the foods and raw materials they cannot grow at home, and adequate markets for their surplus manufactures, has expanded economic nationalism into economic imperialism. This policy is organically connected with

B

a growth of overseas investment, needed on the one
hand for the lucrative disposal of surplus capital
beyond the requirements of home use, on the other
for securing the development of the natural resources
of backward lands for their exclusive or preferential
use, and exclusive or preferential markets for their
manufactured surplus.

As this economic imperialism, primarily a British
policy, spread to a number of other industrially
developed Western powers, the economic conflicts
assumed more and more a political shape, each
government being induced to use its diplomatic,
and in the last resource its armed force for the
protection or assertion of the interest of its own
traders and investors.

Here is the widest area of economic conflict,
qualified but slightly by trade treaties and other
rudiments of an internationalism which as yet has
been brought into no reliable adjustments with the
dominant principle and practice of independent
absolute sovereignty, extended to cover the colonies,
protectorates, and spheres of interest which fall
within the category of empire.

Thus, while it would be foolish to deny that the
economic system contains elements of order in its
industry and markets, it is manifestly failing to
meet efficiently the requirements of modern civilisation. The very fact that everyone becomes increas-
ingly dependent for the satisfaction of economic
needs upon the successful adjustments of industry,
trade, and finance, of a world-wide character, has

brought into stronger relief the failure of these adjustments. An era of confessed national impotence is setting in, and the feebleness of all present attempts at effective economic internationalism is the outstanding challenge to the reason and the will of man.

CHAPTER II

THE MAKING OF INCOMES

It is now widely recognised that if economic havoc and maladjustment attributable to the Great War were repaired, our major problems of waste and injustice would still remain unsolved. It may even be urged that, if the industrial and financial troubles due to the war were healed and the productive capacities of all the civilised peoples were liberated to take full advantage of the recent improvements in technique and organisation, the inability to utilise these enlarged productive powers would be even more conspicuous than it is. Up-to-date modern capitalism under such conditions would exhibit a far larger wastage than is represented by the idle labour and capital at the present time. While, therefore, the war injuries of high tariffs, war debts, reparations, expensive armaments, obstructed emigration, disordered finance, bulk large in the immediate foreground, their very presence has obscured the far more important need of an economic government capable of coping with the more permanent evils of a disordered economic system.

The difficulty here is a state of mind incapable of understanding the nature of the problem, chiefly because it is unwilling to try to understand. It is unwilling because what it deems to be its personal and group interests block the way. "In the absence of pas-

sion and self-interest man is not indisposed to justice."
And when self or group interest is strongly realised,
passion is always present and confuses thinking.

The doctrines and principles that emerge from
passion-laden thinking are worth some consideration
in any attempt at envisaging economic government.
Two 'states of mind' prevalent in all classes are
obstructive to any sound understanding of the
economic situation.

The first is the state of mind towards personal
rights of property, well expressed in letters admitted
to *The Times* from well-to-do persons who deplore
the confiscatory taxation to which their incomes
and property are subjected for expenditure in social
services for the benefit of other people. The assumption, often expressed with the utmost *naïveté*, is that
they themselves, by their own skill, knowledge,
enterprise, industry, and thrift, have *made* the
fortunes which they possess, and that the claim of a
government to take a large share of them by process
of taxation for public purposes is an act of legalised
robbery. Or if they have not *made* these fortunes
themselves, their relatives have made them by the
use of their personal activities and have exercised
the 'right' to bequeath the property to them.

In either case it belongs to them by right of
personal productivity, and for a government to take
any part of it, without their consent, for the benefit
of other people, is only little less immoral than if a
mob took it by violent plunder.

Those who write these letters are perfectly sincere

both in the views they express and in their indigna-
tion. But while most of them belong to the conven-
tionally 'educated' classes, it never enters their
heads to question the validity of their prime assumption that they themselves or their fathers have 'made'
these fortunes. A. is a successful industrialist who has
built up and conducted a profitable business from
which he draws a large income. This income is due
to his enterprise, skill, and industry. Others, no doubt,
have helped him to produce the goods upon the sale
of which his profits depend. But he pays these others
their market value in salaries and wages as he pays
all other costs of production. The bulk of the money
he receives from the sale of his product goes in defray-
ing these costs. Any surplus, i.e. profit, belongs to
him as entrepreneur and capitalist. If others are
shareholders in his enterprise, part of the profit
'belongs' to them. They have made it by the use of
their capital, or the skill of their investment. This is
how the affair appears to him.

But the growing tendency in business is for the
active entrepreneur to borrow most of the money
capital he requires at fixed interest. On this basis it
seems clearer than ever that the large income and
fortune which a prospering business secures for him
is of his own making. Indeed, he can often trace it to
particular acts of skilled judgment and enterprise
upon his part, and he is conscious that any error of
judgment upon his part might have converted his
profit into a loss.

What, then, is the fallacy in his conviction that his

fortune is of his own personal making? It is this. Let it be granted that his skill and judgment, in equipping his works with the best up-to-date plant and in organising production, markets, and finance in the best possible manner, enable him to enlarge his output of the goods he makes. Something else is necessary in order that he may make a large income out of the profitable sale of these goods. In the first place, if other industrialists in his line of business are as able as he is, they may be increasing the output of their plant as rapidly as he, in which case the enlargement of his total supply of these goods upon the market may lead to a large fall in prices and in profits. Thus the income he receives depends to a considerable extent not upon what he does, but upon what others are doing in his line of business. So much for the 'supply' side of the determination of his price and profit. But far more important is the fact that his real income, the command over the general body of goods and services which his money income represents, depends upon the productive operation of all the other industries throughout the world whose products come into comparison with his by means of money and market prices. For this real income, or profit, which he thinks to be of his exclusive 'making,' expands or contracts to an indefinite extent with the expansion or contraction of other goods which compose the 'demand' for the particular goods towards the supply of which he contributes.

Turning from income to property, the capitalised form of ownership, the absurdity of the contention that either personal or real property is personally or really made by its owner is not less apparent. Most modern property consists of shares, or bonds, or other pieces of paper, the value of which is based upon the estimated future earnings or profits of some industrial, commercial, or financial business. These values are liable to fluctuate with every change in the current market for the goods or services the business produces, or with the public confidence in the future of the enterprise. Such property may be worth twice as much, or half as much, next year as it is now, without any action on the part of its owner. Yet the property owner, though aware of these changes due to the conduct of others, is apt to regard his stocks and shares as a fixed property, because the nominal value inscribed on the share certificates does not change, and he regards claims of taxing authorities as invasions upon his rightful ownership. He does not recognise the part played by the economic community in making and changing the amount of his property.

If, however, we regard, as we must, this economic system as 'social' in its operation, we come to the conclusion that A.'s income or fortune, which he imagines himself to have made, is in reality determined or made by the activities of the whole economic system operating through the machinery of markets.

This is, of course, an elementary lesson in economic science. But it has been necessary to set it out explicitly because it is almost universally ignored by members of the owning classes, who denounce alike the encroachment of the State and of organised labour upon the wealth which they have 'made,' or received from those who 'made' it.

This curious power of self-interest to stifle reason is, of course, not peculiar to a capitalist class. Landowners who have made 'big money' by developing a piece of land, which they have either inherited or bought cheap, owing to a shrewd perception of the growing value which its situation and the growth of population in its neighbourhood was likely to bring, hold the same conviction that their 'enterprise' and capital expenditure upon roads have created all the increment in land values that ensues upon this development. It is necessary, however, to discriminate this case from that of industrial profits. For this interpretation of the rights of private ownership in land values has long ago been repudiated not only by 'economists,' but by a large proportion of the business classes, who are quite unable to see any analogy or similarity in the determination of land values and the profits of industrial undertakings.

Still more interesting is the attitude of labour on the subject. What I may term the normal trade union position, as distinguished from the socialist, rests upon the assumption that brain and manual labour are the sole producers of wealth, and, distinguishing profits from managerial salaries, regards profits as a rightful fund for payment of higher wages in the particular business or industry. From the Ricardian doctrine that labour is the source of value they deduce the doctrine that labour has really made the profits in each particular business and is morally entitled to absorb them in wage-rises. It is perhaps less surprising that workers, whose business outlook is as a rule narrowly restricted, should allow immediate self-interest to lead them into this error, than for capitalists who must be aware of the play of wider economic forces determining the special values which interest them. But the labour movement is heavily embarrassed by the feeble grasp of the social determination of values on the part of many of its leaders. One would suppose that recent events must make the lesson plain to the meanest intelligence. Perhaps the simplest cases are those of workers upon or in the earth. The number of bushels of wheat grown on a farm may be regarded as the product of the labour and skill of the farmer, with due regard to the fertility of the soil. Or the number of tons of coal gotten by a hewer in a coal-mine may reasonably appear to be his personal product (other conditions being taken for granted). But the *value* of a bushel of wheat or a ton of coal, which is what the farmer and the miner are really concerned with, the real payment for their toil, depends upon the price the market secures to them, or in the last resort upon the comparison between the value of a unit of wheat or coal and units of all other products of national and world industry.

I need not labour this social determination of values further. But the failure to grasp it and to apply it to the problems I have cited is a chief source of the conflicts, wastes, and injustices of the economic system. Until the claims of the individual worker, the industrial group, and the economic community (national and international) can be brought into reasonable and equitable adjustment by some machinery of economic government, civilisation must remain an exceedingly precarious process.

Some readers, while agreeing that all incomes are socially determined, will be disposed to hold that this social determination tends to pay every man what he is worth to society. Common parlance attests the prevalence of this belief. Eliminating the special cases of ground and mineral rents, monopolies and 'windfalls,' incomes are believed to be substantially correct measures of the quantity and quality of the services rendered by their recipients in the making of wealth. Though complete equality of opportunity, including easy transfer of brains, capital, and labour, from one employment to another, one place to another, is not attained, there is sufficient competition and mobility to make remuneration conform to the 'worth' of the services for which it is paid. If incomes do not always correspond with the efforts or skill that appear to be involved, or to the utility of services rendered, explanations are found in other conditions of work or life outside the measure of money. The brain-work of a high public official is paid on a much lower level than that of a successful lawyer or business man, but there are compensating factors of security and prestige in the former position. Instances of men rising from the lower ranks of society into the most highly remunerated positions in the business world are sufficiently numerous to support the belief that brains and grit can always 'make good,' regardless of the obvious truth that the cases of those who fail to 'make good,' however numerous, necessarily remain unknown. As·for the wide discrepancies of income, they are usually explained by the fact that certain acts of judgment, skilled calculation or audacity, on the part of men in key positions, are often 'productive' in a sense and a degree that are hidden from ordinary recognition. The invention or adoption of a new process, the elimination of some source of waste, the development of a new market, may make so large an increase in the productivity of capital and labour that a trifling percentage of this value accruing to the inventor or the entrepreneur may make him a millionaire. The high remuneration of leading lawyers or doctors in London or New York is commonly regarded as in some sense a just measure of the skill and knowledge contained in their advice, notwithstanding the fact that professional skill at least as good fetches very much smaller pay in Germany or Sweden. In each of these cases the man is said to get 'as much as he is worth.' But a little reflection shows that 'what he is worth' only means 'what he can get' under the circumstances of his special market.[1]

[1] The naïve assumption that somehow personal merit underlies and is attested and even measured by business success is a noteworthy example of defective mentality. It is conveyed in the childish wisdom of the couplet:

> "He put in his thumb and pulled out a plum,
> And said, What a good boy am I"

—not lucky, but personally meritorious!

But what applies to highly skilled work of business and professional men applies also to the grading of wages throughout the economic system. Does any sound measure either of the utility or the needs of various classes of wage-earners determine that a compositor or a plasterer shall receive a payment for his week's work three times that of a skilled farm labourer? Labour in sheltered occupations in this country notoriously receives a higher rate of pay per unit of time, effort, product, needs, or any measure you choose to apply, than labour in unsheltered occupations. Increasing recognition of the unfairness of such scales of pay is corroding the efficiency of the economic system. As trade intercourse increases between nations living on widely different standards of consumption, the sense of the 'unfair' competition of goods produced by 'sweated' or 'forced' labour further inflames this discontent.

Analysis shows that the labour market from top to bottom throughout the economic system distributes income with no regard to equity or humanity. The intervention of governments in most civilised countries does something to guarantee minimum wages, or to supplement them by 'social services,' while it reduces the higher incomes by graduated taxation. But these alleviating circumstances do not go far to meet the gravamen of the charge that earned incomes are based upon no principle of equity. The three defensible measures of an equitable distribution, efforts, products, needs, are all disregarded, excepting so far as they affect the 'pulls' of labour markets. It is economic force, exercised either individually or collectively, in processes of bargaining that determines rates of pay and incomes. Behind the sometimes amicable processes of bargaining between a federation of employers and a trade union for the fixing of wage-rates stand two determining considerations: first, the fact that, in the event of a continued strike or lock-out, the workers suffer starvation, the masters a monetary loss; secondly, the clear knowledge on the part of both masters and men that this is the situation.

But though in all markets for the sale of brain or manual labour, skilled or unskilled, equity, humanity, and reason contribute very little towards the fixation of prices, it is sometimes supposed that in the markets for the other factors of production, and especially in the markets for commodities, competition is normally fair and reasonable. Prices are supposed to be determined by 'the law of supply and demand,' a phrase which seems to give a security for the necessity if not for the justice of the price. What presumption of justice, however, appertains to a 'market' and its 'price' implies that the buyers and the sellers respectively, as bargaining groups and individuals, are equally equipped with bargaining power, and that the price struck thus brings an equal gain or good to each. There are cases which satisfy these conditions, when all the would-be buyers and the would-be sellers (representing supply and demand) have an equal knowledge of the conditions of the market, equal available resources for holding out for a satisfactory

price, and when the price fixed divides the gains of
the deal upon a fifty-fifty basis. But such instances
are so abnormal as to be almost irrelevant in con-
sidering the innumerable varieties of actual markets.
Nor can we draw much comfort from the reflection
that, though the gains may be unequal, both parties
to an act of sale must make some gain. The bargain
of a starving man with the baker, of a needy peasant
with a money-lender, of a shopkeeper with the ground
landlord, of a dealers' food-ring with the retailer or
the consumer, of the small business man with his
banker—such bargains of varying stringency, taken
by themselves, bring a gain to the weaker as well as
to the stronger bargainer. Indeed, the man who thus
pays an extortionate sum for his life, or for his source
of livelihood, may be said to make the greater gain.
For "All that a man hath will he give for his life."
But the iniquity and oppression of such bargains
are manifest. It may be said that the cases cited are
those of abuse of monopoly power, and that when a
competitive market exists, substantial equality and
equity are secured. To this I would reply that a considerable number of markets are conducted on terms
of quasi-monopoly, one party, the sellers or the
buyers, possessing a much stronger power of 'holding
out' than the other, either by conscious combination
or by individual strength. The labour market, under
most conditions, is, of course, a striking example.
But even when fairly free competition exists both
among sellers and buyers, the difference of urgency to
sell or to buy among the competitors on each side

will result in a market price which, though it secures some gain to all, distributes the volume of gain very unequally on both sides, some sellers getting a much higher price than they would have been willing to sell at, others finding in that price a bare inducement to sell, while among the buyers a similar inequality of gain is found in accordance with the greater or less importance of striking a bargain at such a price.

If we could grade all buying and selling processes, from the extreme case of monopoly of a necessity to the freest competition of buyers and sellers for a popular[1] luxury, we should find that nowhere did the price distribute equally or equitably the gain of the marketing process. In no case is the justice other than 'rough.'

Business life, therefore, so far as it centres round market arrangements for buying or selling labour, ability, capital goods, land-uses, consumable commodities, is essentially a selfish exercise of economic force. Everyone seeks to get as much and give as little as he can. Even were it true that this conscious enlightened selfishness worked out to a social harmony, the method is morally degrading. But we now see that it does not so work out. Neither group combination nor individual competition, nor the present conjunction of the two, gives economic, moral, or intellectual satisfaction. Waste, unreason, moral conflict everywhere abound.

[1] I use this term because most markets for high luxuries, such as art products, rare books, fine sites, professional or artistic merit or prestige, are conducted on the most restricted forms of competition.

Thus we reach two conclusions which, if admitted, should be deeply disconcerting to those who hitherto have acquiesced in the working of our economic system as substantially just, reasonable, and efficient. If it is true, upon the one hand, that nobody has any equitable claim to his 'income,' on the ground that he has 'made' it, or given an equivalent amount of personal service, while, on the other hand, the social instrument of its distribution, the markets, completely selfish in the personal motives that rule their working, are unreasonable, unjust, and inhumane in the apportionment of the gains of industry, an exceedingly strong presumptive case is made out for trying to bring these instruments and operations of industry and of markets under the conscious collective control of human will.

C

CHAPTER III

'FORCED LABOUR' AND 'THE RIGHT TO WORK'

It is worth while pausing here to examine the intense resentment aroused in this country by the term 'forced labour' and its economic implications. If we ask whether everyone ought not to make some contribution to society in the shape of useful service in return for his upkeep, the reply of almost all would be in the affirmative. A few might put in a qualifying clause in favour of those in possession of 'independent means,' but under pressure they would usually contend that these exceptional persons performed voluntary services suited to their 'station in life.' In general it is an accepted moral principle that every man should have to work for his living. This principle is endorsed by the most respectable authority. "In the sweat of thy face shalt thou eat bread." "If any man will not work, neither shall he eat." In a primitive agricultural community, such a maxim is a statement rather of natural necessity than of moral obligation. Yet a moral obligation it is seen to be when examined in the light of social ethics. What, then, is the gap between an admission that everyone ought to work and the right of society to see that he does work?

What is wrong with 'forced labour'? In seeking an answer to this question, it may be well to distinguish the humanitarian from the economic objection, though for controversial purposes the two are usually confounded. When we are asked to refuse admission to imported products of forced labour, the gravamen of the charge is that this labour cost is unduly depressed by the unfree conditions under which the work is done. Though the workers may not be 'slaves' or even prisoners, they are not in a position to refuse to work upon the terms imposed by their employers. 'Forcing' is of various kinds: sometimes the instrument is a monetary tax, a head or hut tax, only to be paid by performing wage-labour for outside employers; sometimes it is the arbitrary power of a tribal chief, evoked by the threats or bribes of 'labour agents'; sometimes it is a 'corvee' or other direct governmental compulsion; sometimes the 'peonage' of men kept in debt to a company's store. Physical, legal, or moral compulsion is brought to bear to get labour that could not otherwise be got, and to get it on terms dictated by the employer. Much cruelty and deceit is usually involved in such transactions. Men are taken away from their family and land to work under strange distant masters with whom they cannot bargain; no choice is given them as to the kind of work they shall do or the conditions under which they shall do it. Family life suffers havoc from their absence; the population itself is gradually depleted both by the reduction of males and by the high mortality under 'forced labour.'

What is the essential difference between forced labour and the so-called free labour of an ordinary

wage-system? The proletarian is compelled to work
for an employer. He cannot work for himself, for
he is not the owner of land, machinery, and raw
materials necessary for most productive processes.
His choice of the kind of work he shall do, and
of his employers, is narrowly limited. As a rule
he must find a job in the trade predominant in the
town where he is born and bred, or in some occupation subsidiary to it. With push and energy he may
seek other employment elsewhere, but his choice of
trade and his mobility are very limited. The wages,
hours, and other terms of employment are imposed
on him by an individual agreement with an economically stronger master, or by a collective bargain
made by the body of workers in a trade with the
body of employers. In either case he has little
personal choice. He must work on conditions prescribed by others. He is not free in the sense that a
peasant working for a livelihood upon the soil, or
even for the sale of his produce in a local market,
is free.

What destroys his 'freedom' is not merely the fact
that he has not the land, tools, or materials in his
own possession, but that the work accessible to him
is a particular niche in a single process of an elaborate
series of processes contributing to the making of a
single sort of product. In a word, it is division of
labour that is the 'forcing' factor. Most workers
would prefer some variety in their work, but they
cannot get it. This compulsion, though proceeding
from a system rather than a single master-will, is

none the less a cancelling of liberty. Man becomes 'the slave of the machine' is the ordinary expression in the case of most workers, whether the machine is a physical structure or an office of clerks or salesmen.

Now this obligation to do a particular sort of work for society imposes an obligation on society and a corresponding right upon the individual. This is called 'the right to work,' or, in other words, a claim upon society to provide him with the opportunity to earn a living. Since society is his ultimate employer, it is clearly the duty of society to see that his immediate employer finds him work on terms adequate to maintain him in efficiency, or, failing that, to provide public employment out of public revenue. This is a plain statement of the duty of the State, the economic representative of society, towards the unemployed. He has a right to demand work, it has an obligation to supply it. Unemployed benefit, the dole, is not a fulfilment of this obligation. It has, indeed, its proper place. When there is good reason to believe that the stoppage of employment is a brief temporary condition, it may be well to keep men waiting for the return of normally full employment, instead of drafting them into alien occupations. But the 'right' of the worker to demand work on reasonable terms, and the correlative obligation of the organised community to provide it, are basic conditions of a civilised government. When experience proves that privately ordered industry cannot work without long periods of human waste upon a growing scale of magnitude, the utilisation of that waste for purposes of the production of public wealth must become a first consideration of the government. If public works, as is perhaps likely, cannot be made fully remunerative, when measured by the values of outside private industry, the difference must evidently be made up by taking 'surplus' incomes from private industry, in order to defray the net costs of its human wastage, which obligation the current operation of capitalism enables it to evade.

If, as some economists hold, the normal tendency of the 'new economic revolution' is a constantly growing 'economy of labour' by a substitution of machine-power for direct human labour, the growth of an ever-larger communal production will be forced upon each Western nation by the inadequate employment which the capitalist system can provide. The State cannot see workers starve, it cannot keep them in continuous idleness, it must therefore develop a system of productive employment which shall supplement the capitalist system, and possibly displace it over a wide range of industry.

This admission of the 'right to work' carries with it, of course, the assumption that society must decide what work each man shall do. So we get round again to the case of 'forced labour,' with a qualification. The recent administration of the 'dole' has already to some extent disposed of the untenable position that an unemployed person in receipt of relief may refuse work in another occupation or another place. In other words, the right to work does not carry the additional right to choose your own

work or your work-place. If, as is the fact, you are
working for the good of the community, you must let
the community decide what you can do best. There is,
however, a qualifying circumstance, viz. the consideration that a man will probably do more and
better work in a trade that is congenial to him than
in one that he dislikes. In some ways he is a better
judge than any outside authority, not only of his
tastes but of his aptitudes. It would, therefore, be
sound public policy to consult his taste as far as
practicable. But since most work is not in itself
agreeable and the relative agreeability or disagree-
ability can seldom be known without actual experience, it is clear that personal choice must be strictly
limited. Moreover, there will be obvious incompati-
bility between the tastes of workers and the requirements of society. There must remain, therefore, in the
hands of the public authority a right to enforce
the terms of public employment, though it is in the
interest of the public that these terms shall be as
liberal as possible, so as to secure as far as possible
the consent of the governed. But the individual 'right
to work' carries as its correlative the right of society
to allot to each the work which it is best for society
that he should do, and to fix the wages and other
conditions of his employment. If he cannot make a
satisfactory bargain with a capitalist employer, he
must accept public work under conditions prescribed
by the State in 'forced labour.'

CHAPTER IV

CLAIMS UPON SURPLUS INCOME, PERSONAL
AND COMMUNAL

If it were recognised by all thinking men and women that the incomes they received for their personal efforts in production were only to a slight extent determined by the quantity and quality of their efforts, and chiefly by the efforts of other producers contributing to the same supply of products and to the efforts of producers in all other industries whose incomes constituted the demand for their products, this understanding would revolutionise their attitude towards taxation and the 'social services' upon which public revenue is expended. For they would perceive that taxation was not an invasion of their property rights, a forcible seizure of wealth which they have made, but a claim exercised by the State as representing the contribution which economic society had made towards 'their' incomes. In other words, the justification for taxation would no longer rest upon needs of revenue for the maintenance of public order, but would extend to cover the whole of that part of income and wealth which could rightly be regarded as the product of social activities. Here two objections may be raised. It may be urged that the so-called 'social' determination through 'markets' is nothing other than the activities of individual producers and purchasers. I would reply that the impact of these particular activities upon prices and through prices on real incomes is incapable of separate assessment and cannot be resolved into a multitude of individual claims. Moreover, it is not true that a social force or effort is the mere aggregate of individual forces and efforts. Organised society as a unitary whole supports the economic system and helps every member in the performance of his function.

Taxation, thus viewed, is the resumption by society of an income due to it as a productive instrument, and needed by it, as the individual needs his share, for maintenance and vital progress. The share thus due to society need not, of course, be taken by taxation. In a wholly or partially 'socialised' community the distribution of the product, or its value, will be such as directly to assign to society the net profits of each enterprise after meeting the expenses of production upon a basis of the personal efficiency of all producers. Such profits, or surplus, would be available either for the reduction of prices to the consumer of the product, or for the improvement of this or some other economic public service, or for the extension of social services that are non-economic in their direct intent, such as health, education, and recreation.

Almost all modern economic nations have been 'socialising' themselves along these two paths, running certain basic services by publicly owned or controlled instruments, and enlarging and improving 'social' services, partly by expending the gains

from socialised industries, but mainly by taxing
surplus elements of private incomes and inherited
wealth.

Our analysis of markets, as social instruments for
the determination of values and the distribution of
industrial gains, showed how what we here term 'the
surplus' was distributed not according to any canons
of justice or utility, but according to the strength of
'pull,' the economic force of the buyers and sellers,
collectively and individually regarded. It is this
unfair and wasteful apportionment of industrial gains
or real income by the ill-ordered social processes of
bargaining in markets that constitutes the need for
a genuinely conscious economic government. For
while we have dwelt chiefly upon the unfairness
and inhumanity of the conduct of industry and the
distribution of incomes, these charges, always valid
in every age and country, are now reinforced by a
growing realisation that this unfair and inhumane
system will no longer work satisfactorily even from
the standpoint of the financially and industrially
powerful classes. The system, indeed, works so
wastefully, with so much friction and stoppage, that
many of the owning classes find their surplus incomes
shrinking. I need not here discuss the causes of this
new trouble, for in its scale and its duration it is
new. War and post-war dislocations, industrial and
financial troubles, the growth of tariffs and other
economic barriers, the failure of wage-rates to adjust
themselves to falling prices, and of gold to respond
in output to the requirements of industry and

credit—to these and other factors in our present troubles economic doctors ascribe very diverse values.

But the nature of the economic disease itself is not a matter of dispute. With existing plant and power, natural resources, labour, and managerial knowledge, the world could produce at least twice as much wealth *per capita* as it is actually producing, without undue strain upon human energy. For the volume of unemployed labour, huge though it is, is no adequate measure of the wastage. The slowing down of many processes, the limitation of output by organised capital, the corresponding ca' canny of labour, the continuous drift from the productive into the distributive trades, in excess of any real demand, add greatly to the waste. But perhaps an even greater source of waste is the failure of attempts on the part of the depressed trades to re-equip themselves with up-to-date technique and organisation. The reasons for this failure are two. First, the unwillingness of a large number of separate and hitherto competing firms to enter into common arrangements for buying and selling and so to organise their producing units as to avoid overlapping and other wastes. Suspicion, jealousy, and sheer inertia are chief retarding forces. Secondly, though investment capital and bank credit are available in abundance for any business proposition which can show a reasonable prospect of effecting sales at a profitable price, the downward trend of prices has made it exceedingly difficult for would-be producers to show that further use of capital upon technique could enable them to make a profit upon their enlarged output.

Everywhere we are brought up against the obstinate fact that the productive powers of capital and labour are excessive, in the sense that any attempt to operate them fully creates a glut and a stoppage because markets for goods do not expand to keep pace with productivity. The waste of cyclical fluctuations with their long spells of un- and under-employment is manifestly attributable to this maladjustment. But this is only a restatement of the problem, not an explanation, still less a solution. There are various explanations, the chief of which are, (1) a failure of the quantity of money, or purchasing power, to keep pace with the expanding needs of commerce by reason of a shortage of the gold supply; (2) the high wages and the shorter hours which, taken along with the burden of taxation on incomes and industry, make it unprofitable to operate a large proportion of existing plant and labour; (3) a distribution of the general income which in normal times causes an attempt to save and put into increased capital a larger proportion of the income than is required to turn out the quantity of final commodities that can be bought by the income that is spent.

I do not wish here to discuss the respective value of these explanations, but only to insist that all of them admit the magnitude of the maladjustment and the inability of the economic system to effect a cure without constructive planning on a national and a world scale. There are, of course, economists and statesmen who think nothing can usefully be done except to wait for the swing of the pendulum, the turn of the tide, or the clouds to roll by. These maladjustments, distressing as they are and wasteful as they seem, are for them the expressions of natural laws, and seen in this light belong to a true economy of industrial evolution. The clumsy attempts of governments or other social bodies to interfere with them will only make matters worse!

But this is a foolish surrender to the forces of un-reason, a claim to withdraw from man's rational control the largest sphere of his collective conduct, to assign to industry a reign of law which nobody would think of assigning to religion, politics, art, science, sport, or any other activity of man. The old *laissez-faire* had a sort of reason in its policy. It believed that the reasonable judgment upon which each man based his economic conduct would better serve the common good than the obstructive inter-ferences of governments. This may have been sound reasoning for the time. But this new *laissez-faire*, the denial of all utility to collective planning, is at bottom a cover for the fears and greeds of the classes whose property interests may be assailed by attempts to put industry upon a more reasonable and more equitable footing. They evoke the rigours of economic laws in defence of the existing disorder, because they are unwilling to submit the concepts and institutions of property to damaging scrutiny.

The acute French critic, M. André Siegfried, has lately dwelt upon the special faculty of the British for blinding their eyes, not consciously but instinctively, to any line of reasoning or any set of facts which seriously disturb their convenience or dignity. It cannot, therefore, be assumed with confidence that what are here deemed to be irrefutable criticisms upon the working of the economic system, will be absorbed by any considerable section of those who are interested in not understanding them or in not recognising their validity. Nor is this convenient blindness confined to the capitalist and wealthy classes. It is equally difficult to get workers in the sheltered high-wage occupations to recognise the possibility, or indeed certainty, that their higher earnings must to a considerable extent entail reductions in the real wages of the workers in the unsheltered trades.

*   *   *   *   *

But is it impossible to formulate principles for the conduct of industry which by their evident reasonability and equity will gradually, or even quickly, release increasing numbers of decent-minded men and women from the grip of prejudice and self-interest and lead them to the acceptance of a new economic order? An approach towards the discovery of such principles is to be found in the familiar communist maxim: "From each according to his capacity, to each according to his needs." Each half of this maxim makes a separate appeal to reason. A well-ordered economy would get from each member the best and largest service he was fit by nature, training, and circumstances to render. This economy would

yield the largest and best product at the lowest
human cost. The distribution of this product "according to needs," or capacity to use, would ensure the
largest human utility or vital service from its
consumption. But though each half makes a separate
convincing appeal, the appeal of the whole is far
less convincing. The principle may operate success-
fully in the close economy of a good family, or even
within a small religious community. But it would not
work, it is held, in Western civilisation, on the larger
scale and with the lesser contacts, of a town, a
nation, or the world economic system. Altruism, or
communal feeling, is not strong enough in most men
to evoke their best personal efforts of production
unless they get for their separate use or enjoyment
a share of the product measured not by their personal needs, but by what seems to them to be the
amount and quality of their effort, or its result.
There still persists a strong belief in the equity of
payment by result, though, as we see, it is based upon
a fallacious disregard of the social determination of
value. This false sense of equity is, however, nothing
else than a cover for the undeniable fact that men
will not work their best unless they are paid for doing
so, a doctrine in antagonism with 'payment according
to needs.' Some compromises on both sides of this
difficulty are possible. On the physical plane, at any
rate, there is some correspondence between effort and
need, between the output of productive energy and
the intake of food. In some higher kinds of work a
fairly large personal income and expenditure may be

required to provide the seclusion, travel, and other experience enabling a man to put forth his best intellectual or creative productivity. But it cannot be held that these considerations justify the wide discrepancies between the incomes of the rich and the poor in any society, or meet the obvious objection that most poor people do far more disagreeable work than most rich people, and do it under circumstances detrimental to life itself, as is reflected in the vital statistics of occupations.

Another qualification is found in the fact that respectability or prestige, skill, the possession of a sense of power and some genuine regard for public or personal service, count to some extent in certain occupations as substitutes for higher pay. Indeed, in the higher public offices of a State or municipality, and sometimes in private corporate bodies, the 'needs' basis of payment obtains recognition in the sense of 'keeping up a position' in society.

But such qualifications only modify to a slight extent the general acceptance of a system of distribution of income based not on 'needs,' but upon productive effort or output as valued by market strength. The owner of any scarce factor of production is paid according to the socially determined price of its scarcity, which has indeed some relation to its utility but no assignable relation to its cost in terms of human effort.

How far can any principle or policy be found for moderating or overcoming the obvious waste and injustice of this distribution? Must some people

always continue to give out more than their share
of productive effort, while others give out less, or
none? Must some receive more than they need for
their true use and enjoyment, others less? There is no
complete answer to such questions. For in the first
place, as we see, there is no accurate measure of the
part played by individual effort and social effort
respectively in making the value of any product.
Measuring the physical output may furnish some
rough estimate of the energy given out by the worker,
though not necessarily of his effort, for workers vary
in strength and endurance. But, as we have seen,
the payment for such work, the real wage in terms
of purchasing power, is determined by the aggregate
efforts and outputs of all who contribute to the supply
of and the demand for this physical output. There is
no way of measuring his particular contribution to
the market value of the product.

There is, however, an approach towards equity and
economy in an interpretation of the principle that a
labourer is worthy of his hire—that is, he ought to
receive what will support him in continuing to do his
work. Such support, however, must not be interpreted
merely in terms of subsistence or even of physical
efficiency for himself and his family. It must be such
as to evoke his best work. In other words, it must be
an incentive to his full productivity, neither more nor
less. 'The economy of high wages' has always kept
this principle in view. It has always denounced the
folly as well as the sin of sweating. On the other hand,
it has recognised that any sudden large rise of wages,

due to some temporary scarcity of labour or other cause, is usually ill-spent and often conducive to waste of time or other inefficiency. The *justum pretium* will vary from age to age, from job to job. But at any time and for any work it means that rate of pay which suffices to evoke the best work of each worker.

But what applies to wage-labour applies to every sort of labour and to the service rendered in industry by the owner of any other factor in production. Everywhere the test question is what is the least payment necessary to evoke and maintain the service which each factor is able to render. This doctrine of incentive is obnoxious to strict equalitarianism. It means that this man will get more than that man, not because he needs it, or deserves it in any moral sense, but because he is stronger or cleverer than the other man and will not put out his full strength or cleverness unless he is paid to do so.

Applied to the higher and rarer qualities of human work, the managerial and organising capacity of a great business leader, the finer qualities of professional skill, the creative power of the painter or the dramatist, we seem to encounter a defence of payment often exorbitant and bearing no relation towards needs. The man who can make millions by an astute business deal, the surgeon who can rack-rent wealthy patients for an operation, the film star who can get his £1,000 a week upon a contract—does the fact that such payments can be extorted imply that they are necessary incentives to the performance of this skilled work? Here caution is necessary to a right reply. In each of these cases, *accepting the market as it stands*, it may be held that these large sums are necessary payments. There is a scarcity of these first-rate capacities, and the demand for their particular services is so intense or so widespread that their owners can loot the public, precisely as can the owner of some highly favoured ground in a growing city. This remuneration is necessary in the sense that *in the circumstances* the recipients of these large payments are able to insist on getting them. But if the circumstances were different, they would consent to do the same skilled work for one-tenth or one-hundredth of the price. What is meant by "different circumstances"? Well, on the side of supply, if the educational and other opportunities in the country furnished a larger crop of equally well-equipped and skilful brains in these fields, the competition of these with one another would considerably abate the price. On the side of demand, if incomes were more equally divided so that few rich people could afford the fees of the reputable surgeons or lawyers, or engage in great financial operations, the prices for such services would go down.

If we follow out this line of thought, we see that what a man can actually get in his market is no true measure of the incentive socially necessary to secure his efficient services. It is just one more illustration of the determination of incomes according to 'pulls.' What applies to wages, fees, and salaries, applies with even greater force to payments made to

the owners of capital. The interest or dividends that
constitute the payment of capital are the prices paid
to those whose saving involves considerable self-
sacrifice in restricting their current expenditure.
In economic language the 'marginal saver' determines
the price. If 5 per cent. must be paid to him in order
to induce him to postpone some present benefit or
enjoyment, it must be paid to all the other savers
who would consent to save for a smaller payment or
even for no payment. If it be regarded as a necessary
incentive to the marginal saver, it is evidently an
excessive or wasteful one as applied to all the others.
A great deal of saving is regardless of rate of interest,
consisting of the almost automatic accumulation
of the unspent surplus of the rich—unspent because
all their felt wants have been fully satisfied. The large
amount of savings accumulated in good times by
business companies as 'reserves' must doubtless be
accredited with some expectation of future 'earnings'
or dividends as a motive. But a fall in the expected
rate of interest does not act appreciably as a check
upon such saving, or a rise increase it. Even in the
case of the savings of middling or working-class
incomes it is not certain that a rise in the rate of
interest would evoke a larger aggregate of saving.
For those who save in order to make some definite
provision for old age or other emergency would be
disposed to save less, if interest was likely to remain
high, because a smaller amount would make the
provision they require. At any rate there is no ground
for holding that the price of saving conforms at all

closely to 'the law of supply' which assumes that the amount of supply will vary directly and closely with the price.

Add to this analysis the case of payments made under the head of 'profits'to entrepreneurs, financiers, speculators, and middlemen in various markets, and you will find no real correspondence between the incomes thus 'earned' and the incomes essential to evoke what services these men render. Such payments, whether classed as rewards of enterprise, as profits, windfalls, or what not, have no definite or rational relation either to the amount of services rendered or to the sums that would suffice to evoke these services. Because a Rockefeller or a Ford can get a hundred million pounds out of producing and selling oil or motor-cars, it does not follow that this is a necessary incentive to the exercise of his business ability. He would have exercised this ability just as well if he could have got out of it one million instead of a hundred.

Now our principle of equity and economy requires that so far as possible individual incomes should correspond with necessary incentives. One class of payment I have reserved to the end, because it presents the principle at its plainest, viz. the rents paid for the use of land. As distinguished from payments for capital sunk in improvement and development, these rents do nothing to increase the supply of land or its natural resources. Where they are under private ownership a nominal rent may be a necessary incentive to induce the owner to apply them to their most beneficial use. But virtually the whole body of rents lies outside the category of necessary costs. By general consent of economists they form a 'surplus,' a body of wealth or income upon which a tax will lie without reducing the supply of the article taxed. Virtually the whole of economic rent can be taken for public revenue without disturbance to industry of any kind. No other payment or income is precisely on this footing. But our analysis shows that everywhere in the process of buying and selling, whether of commodities or of the services of labour, capital, and ability, there emerge large elements of a similar surplus, payments not necessary to evoke the efficient use of the factors of production. This surplus consists of every sort of payment in excess of the minimum incentive. This minimum price varies largely with 'circumstances' which, when traced down, amount to equality or inequality of economic opportunity.

In a nation like ours many large payments are made as 'necessary' incentives which need not be made under more equalitarian conditions.

These 'surpluses,' so far as they are not taken by taxation, form the 'irrational' or wasteful factor in our economic system. As income they have no justification, moral or economic. Their low utility for purposes of consumption or enjoyment leads to their accumulation as savings for investment in excess of the requirements and possible uses of the economic system as a whole.

It is sometimes objected that whereas 'costs' are

known and measurable things, 'surplus' is hypo-
thetical or at any rate not susceptible of close
measurement. Even in the case of rents of land, it is
not easy to discriminate between annual land values
and the interest upon 'improvements.' In industrial
and commercial businesses 'costs,' both in the shape of
running expenses and plant upkeep, are continually
fluctuating, while what may be termed 'excess
profits' in the year's net income may contain a provision against low profits or no profits in the next
year. These, no doubt, are real obstacles to the
exact computation of 'surplus.' But they do not
dispose of it as a serviceable concept on which to
base a practicable policy. Every sound taxing system
supposes such a surplus, upon which a tax will lie
without impairing productivity. Progressive taxation
of incomes and properties is only economically
justifiable on the assumption that the larger the
income or property, the greater the element of
surplus value it contains. Though it is often held that
'capacity to pay' is measured by the utility attach-
ing to the income on its expenditure side, rather than
to the excess on the costs side, the two measures
correspond. For the utility from expenditure of high
levels of income bears a close natural relation to
the incentive to produce the goods from the sale of
which such income is derived. What we have termed
the 'surplus' element in income has a low or no
utility for consumption precisely because it is a
payment in excess of any personal services rendered.

This distinction between 'costs' and 'surplus' is

absolutely vital to an understanding of the actual
working of the industrial system and as a basis for
its reform and reconstruction in view of its manifest
breakdown.

It also furnishes the key to what we term the
equitable distribution and use of wealth. For this
composite surplus is economically available for two
purposes. First, for a higher wage and leisure policy
which will raise the standard of life and comfort
for the main body of the people. Secondly, for the
increasing public revenue needed for the growth and
improvement of the communal services which can
secure, enlarge, and enrich the life of the people in
each country and in the world at large.

It is important to recognise that these two uses of
the surplus are complementary and not competitive.
For in most labour movements, and especially in that
of this country, there is danger of a grave misunder-
standing. Organised groups of workers are naturally
apt to accept the view that labour, being the sole
source of wealth, ought to receive the whole of the
product, with such deductions as may be recognised
for the strictly necessary public services and for such
public control of industry as is necessary to secure
their policy of high wages. Each group of workers in
its national or local organisation seeks to apply this
principle for its own separate gain, on the false
assumption that if each trade separately presses for
a policy of higher wages and other improved conditions, this will give due and adequate satisfaction
to the claims of labour as a whole. We have noted

that this separatism is responsible for grave inequali-
ties and conflicts of interest between organised and
unorganised labour, sheltered and unsheltered trades,
agriculture and town industry, within each country,
and the still wider conflicts of nation with nation
in the world of labour.

Socialism, everywhere, encountering this separatist
view, is disposed at first to overstress the principle
that all values are socially produced and that therefore all industry should be directly conducted by the
State or other social government, which, after meeting strict costs of production, should take all profit
or surplus for public revenue to be applied to social
services. But this rigorous state socialism is now
giving place to a better balanced conception of the
industrial system. For it is evident that the workers
in most industries are entitled to demand a larger
share, if not in the value of the product of their
particular industry, at any rate in the value of the
output of the industrial system, for the moulding
of their own standard of life after their personal
patterns. Such enlargement of the individual income
is not an encroachment upon the rights of society
to administer the social income. It is an important
aspect of such social administration. Reconcilement
of these two claims upon the 'surplus' will be found
in the recognition on the part of organised com-
munities that larger liberty of self-expression through
personal expenditure is one essential condition of
industrial democracy, the other being a direct participation by each worker in the control of the business

and industry in which he is engaged. Confining our
attention at present to the income aspect, we shall
perceive that, just in proportion as the body of the
workers in a country gets control of its public policy,
this issue as to how much of the economic surplus
should pass in higher wages, shorter hours, and
better conditions to the several groups of workers,
and how much should be taken as public revenue for
the development of communal services, will achieve
high prominence. There can be no exact criterion for
a just and fruitful apportionment of the surplus
wealth, after due provision has been made for current
efficiency of labour and the necessary provision of
capital for a rising standard of comfort that is
anticipated, for a growing or a stable population.
The apportionment as between personal and public
incomes will rightly depend upon a judgment as to
the relative ability of individuals and public bodies
to make a beneficial use of the money. If, on the one
hand, it is contended that persons alone know
definitely what they want and so are likely to get
more out of the expenditure, on the other hand two
relevant claims will be put forward. The first is that
many of the admitted utilities and amenities from
social services, such as health, education, free
libraries, parks, galleries, etc., cannot be got at all
by private expenditure. They require a constantly
increasing income as the conception of communal life
expands. The second point is that, unpopular as
the claim may seem, while individual recipients of
higher income may know better what they want to

do with the money, it does not follow that what they want is a good or the best use of the money. The chief reason why France is so backward in matters of hygiene, why her death-rate is so much higher than that of most civilised countries, is that public enforcement of hygienic practices is thwarted by a really obstructive neglect of the rules of health by her peasantry. There is in most countries, just in proportion as genuine education advances, a willingness on the part of the people to accept and adopt from officials and experts improvements in ways of living which they would not as individuals have discovered or carried out. Though public services will contain elements of waste and slackness, their continual increase in this and most countries is a testimony to a growth of confidence in the value got out of public expenditure, when the ordinary people believe in the personal honesty and efficiency of administrators.

But there is something else that helps to determine how much of the 'surplus' should go to higher personal incomes, how much to public services. This something is that quality of character which we may call sociability, the willingness and desire to co-operate easily with one's fellows in the performance of common tasks, the enjoyment of common pleasures, and the participation in common enterprises. If it is a permanent trait in our national character that 'islander' means isolation not merely from foreigners but from fellow-countrymen, that every Englishman is an island, that we are proud of being 'bad mixers,' of 'keeping ourselves to ourselves,' of being uncommunicative to strangers, even to neighbours, this quality will assuredly limit the amount of communism we shall admit into our economic system, both on the side of production and of distribution.

How far these distinctions in national character are rooted in some quality of human nature, how far the product of changeable environment and institutions, will be matter of dispute. But, so far as they prevail, they will certainly affect the pace of the growth of communism that is taking place in every civilised country, even perhaps America. But interesting and important as is this relation between the communistic and the individualistic claims upon the surplus, the absorption of this surplus in expenditure for final goods and services is the immediate line of progress. For upon this depends the adjustment between productivity and consumption which is seen to be indispensable for the full utilisation of our new economic powers.

The inequality and inequity of distribution, expressed in the accumulation of excessive payments by economic pulls of favoured persons and groups scattered throughout the industrial system, are seen everywhere to clog the wheels of industry, stop production, spread unemployment and poverty. This is due to a vain and ignorant endeavour to save and invest in increased and improved plants and materials a larger proportion of the total income than can and does function as productive capital. This recurrent malady can only be prevented by an improved application of surplus income to beneficial current expenditure of the workers on the one hand, the community upon the other.

*   *   *   *   *

Thus we are brought back to our starting-point, viz. the resentment felt against taxation on the ground that it is confiscation of income or wealth which 'I have made' and which therefore is 'mine by right.' Our analysis has shown that though 'my' personal activity has in most cases been a contributory factor towards the 'making' of my income or wealth, the whole of economic society has contributed to its value by influencing the supply of it or the demand for it.

Since it is not possible to measure with any true precision the proportionate size of my contribution and that of the economic society of which I am a member, substantial justice is done by alloting to me on the one hand, society upon the other, such payment as will sustain and evoke our maximum efficiency. This is the true distribution according to 'costs,' on the one hand, 'needs' on the other. For if incentives are taken into due account costs will harmonise with needs. The requirements for a larger and richer personality will involve not only an increase of personal income and expenditure, but an increase of communal income and expenditure.

If, by a right adjustment of the claims of the individual and society, provision is thus made for enlargement and enrichment of both, the body of income here termed 'surplus' is absorbed in 'costs of progress.' The problem will be one of the proportionate distribution of what on the static basis is 'surplus' for application along the two lines of progress. And this we have seen will depend largely upon the measure of community or sociality appertaining to the personality.

Where a communist organisation of society exists, the tendency will be for the government to allot to the individual what it deems a sufficient incentive to progressive efficiency, and to apply the residue to strengthening the economic structure and satisfying the economic needs of the community. Under what may still be called the individualist system, taxation direct or indirect, of individual income and wealth will be the normal way in which the State or community claims its share in virtue of its costs and needs. Thus regarded, the public's claim to a part of each man's income or wealth is put upon the same economic and moral footing as that of the man himself. His resentment at what seems a forcible encroachment upon his property is due to a misconception of its origin and causation, supported by the fact that for convenience society does not in most cases claim its share on each separate item of income, but leaves the whole sum for the time being in the taxpayer's possession, asserting the claim to its share in a lump sum later on. By excessive demands upon certain incomes or forms of property, a State may injuriously encroach upon the true costs or pecuniary incentives necessary to make capital, ability, or labour function with full efficiency, so killing the bird that lays the golden eggs. When this happens, mistakes regarding the real incidence of a tax are the usual cause. But, since it is generally recognised by tax experts that the separate bits of 'surplus' as they emerge in markets cannot easily be detected and measured, the usual process is to do rough justice by graduated taxes upon incomes and properties, erring rather on the side of taking too little than too much.

The policy of high wages, co-operative enterprise, and expanding social services has so far been supported on the ground that it transfers what is otherwise an irrational surplus, in excess of the necessary costs of production, from its recipients and applies it to raise the personality of the workers on the one hand, the community on the other. Thus what is otherwise an irrational element in the economic system is rationalised. But the justification of this policy is not exhausted by this consideration of the better uses to which this 'surplus' over costs is put. For, as we have seen, this unearned surplus flowing into excessive money savings, incapable of investment in serviceable capital, is the direct cause of the stoppages of industry, the collapse of prices and the unemployment, classed under the term trade depression. The application of this surplus, the forced gains that come from economic advantage in bargaining, to enlarge the spending power and consumption of the workers and the community, will remedy these chronic maladjustments by raising the aggregate power of consumption to keep pace with every increase of productive power.

To many business men and to some economists it will seem preposterous to propose high wages and high taxes as remedies for unemployment. Even if high direct taxes do not increase costs of production, high wages do, unless accompanied by corresponding increase of labour efficiency and output which in most cases cannot be expected to ensue. To raise wage-rates in a business which can barely meet current costs is seen to be impracticable. And so it is if the policy is tested by application to a single business or even a single trade. For this separatist application does not provide the expansion of demand which alone can validate the policy. If a single business, or a single industry, were to raise its wages, the amount of increased spending power given to its workers would only to a slight extent be applied to purchase more of the goods which this particular business or industry produced. To raise wages in the motor industry or even in the cotton trade would not cause workers in these trades to buy many more motors or cotton goods. So the chief economic justification for high wages, viz. that they furnish a larger market, stimulate production, and reduce overhead costs per unit of product, does not apply, except on a general scale. But if, either by an enlightened agreement among the leaders in most industries or by some State policy of minimum wages, the high-wage policy were simultaneously applied to all or most occupations, the general increase of consuming power and of demand might easily provide a sufficient new fund to meet the higher wage bill out of the reduction in overhead costs due to the full continuous use of the plant and permanent staff, etc.

To disprove this economy of high wages by taking single concrete cases of businesses or trades is precisely analogous to the common protectionist appeal to the gain which a single trade in Birmingham or Sheffield could get by keeping out cheaper foreign goods. To argue from such a case that a general tariff would profit trade as a whole, ignores the fact that protection applied to each other trade reduces the gain to this particular trade by raising the price of their products, and that a zero-point is reached before the tariff is complete.

The folly of a general reduction of wages as a method of reducing costs of production and restoring to the capitalist-entrepreneur his necessary margin of profit has been sufficiently exposed by recent experience. It fails because, though the labour cost per unit of production is reduced, the capital cost is increased by reason of the diminution in output and sales due to the reduced purchasing power of the general body of workers and consumers. The virtue of the high-wage policy consists in the fuller employment given both to capital and labour by the increased demand issuing from labour. It does not, however, follow that the high-wage policy can be applied indiscriminately. Depending, as it does, upon reduction of overhead expenses due to increased

E

sales, its efficacy will vary with the proportion between 'overheads' and other elements of cost. Where, as in the highly developed machine industries, the amount of capital employed per head of labour is large, the waste of overhead charges from stoppages and slowing down is correspondingly great. Such industries will benefit most by a high-wage policy reacting on increased demand for the goods they supply. Other industries with lower overhead charges would benefit less. A rise of, say, 10 per cent. in their wage bill might not be fully compensated by the reduction of overhead charges arising from increased sales and larger output. The application of the high-wage policy ought therefore to take into due account the diverse effects of increasing output upon overhead expenses. Another consideration arises. A rise of real wages, purchasing power of the workers, whether due to higher wage-rates or to a fall in the price-level, will express itself in very different degrees of increased demand for different kinds of commodities. So far as it takes shape in increased purchases of highly standardised goods and services, where expensive machinery plays a predominant part in production, its effect will be to reduce capital costs and to enable more labour to be employed at the higher wage-rate. Since most increases of wages are expended upon such highly standardised goods and services, whether in the shape of clothing or other material comforts and enjoyments, and since it is chiefly in these mechanical industries that depression and unemployment are most acute, the case for high wages as a remedy is exceedingly strong. To increase the proportion of the general income that comes to the wage-earners, whether through high wages, or through the 'divi.' of the co-operative store, or through increasing social services, is the essential condition for the maintenance of full employment in those industries that are most prone to periods of depression and unemployment.

Under such conditions the only waste and unemployment that would occur would be the result of errors in the application of producing power as between industry and industry, some seasonal fluctuations and some temporary wastage from sudden changes in arts of production and the tastes of consumers. The great cyclical collapses would disappear if by this absorption of waste savings the aggregate of consumption kept pace with the aggregate of production. The two related 'irrationals' of our economic system, the unearned, unneeded, and unutilised surplus and the cylical unemployment would disappear together. As no check would then be placed upon the technological and organising improvements of the economic system, the production of wealth would increase enormously, cancelling the absurd under-estimates which economists have based upon statistics of our actual national income, and showing that poverty could be abolished without any miraculous additions to our control over our environment, or any miraculous changes in human mind or morals. The issue is one of applying plainly recognisable policies of equity or fair play to the working of our economic system. In using the words 'plainly recognisable' I may appear to be begging the question. For it is precisely the refusal to recognise such analysis as is here presented that blocks the way. Behind the economic problem lies a psychological or ethical problem, that of getting persons to recognise truths which they deem it to their interest to avoid. This avoidance takes three forms. Some step aside when an inconvenient truth approaches, by an instinctive desire not to meet it. Others look it boldly in the face and pass on. A few controvert and reject it by reasoning, which satisfies their interest-laden minds.

How to get the sense of equity or fair play which prevails in many other spheres of action to focus upon these passionate and disturbing economic questions is thus distinctively a moral issue.

CHAPTER V

INTERNATIONAL ECONOMIC GOVERNMENT

If our nation were a self-sufficing economic area, such a readjustment of the situation by a better distribution and use of incomes might appear convincing. But since Britain's population cannot become self-sufficing, but must continue to depend upon overseas markets for buying and selling, how far does this important fact invalidate the practical policy of reformed distribution here advocated? Can we maintain a higher wage and a higher standard of living within our section of the world economic system than prevails in other sections which are in close commercial relations with us, buying and selling in the same world markets?

At first sight it may seem that an answer may be given to this question by discriminating between our sheltered and our unsheltered trades, between those working almost or quite exclusively for the home market and with a complete possession of that market, and the export trades and other trades subject to the competition of imported goods. Surely, it may be said, a high-wage policy is practicable for our building trades, our railways, our printing trade, our shop-assistants, our public employees, even though it may not be practicable for our textile, metal, furniture, and coal industries. For the validity of a high-wage policy depends upon the effect of high

wages in stimulating an adequate expansion of
demand, and in the unsheltered industries the higher
wage-cost would only stimulate the home demand, so
exerting a smaller effect in reducing overhead costs
than in the industries wholly dependent on home
markets. The net result of high wages in such cases
would be to increase the labour cost per unit of the
product, a bale of cotton, a ton of coal, etc., without
compensating this increased cost by a sufficient
reduction of overhead costs. This being so, our
export trade would shrink, and competing imports
would flow more largely into our markets. In such a
trade as cotton, where some 70 per cent. of the
product normally has gone overseas, a national high-
wage policy would only enlarge the demand for
cotton goods in 30 per cent. of the market, and that
would not suffice to keep the plant and labour in full
employment, reducing overheads to compensate
high wages. In the cheaper branches of the motor-car
industry, on the other hand, a national high-wage
policy might justify itself by stimulating so large
a home demand that 'rationalised' industry would
realise the full economies of standardised production,
winning an increasing proportion of the home and
even of the overseas market.

If, however, we investigate the sheltered occupations as a whole, we shall not find that the higher
wage-rates which prevail in them are always, or
usually, accompanied by such economies of overhead
expenses as enable costs of production and selling
prices to fall so as to increase the volume of employ-

ment of capital and labour in the trade. On the contrary, the relatively high wages of building labour bring dearer housing, in printing, binding, etc., they mean dearer books, in tailoring dearer clothes, etc. Thus the higher wages in these and many other sheltered occupations signify a reduction in the real wages of the unsheltered lower-paid workers, diminishing their demand for the dearer goods and services of the unsheltered trades, and so disabling the latter from enjoying the advantages of a larger home market.

But this reduction of the real wages of unsheltered industries, on account of the high wages of the sheltered, does not signify such reduction in money wages as might put our costs of production on an equal level with those in lower-waged continental countries competing with us in the world market. On the contrary, it is just these high prices for housing, clothing, travel, public services, etc., that make it more difficult to get wages and other costs in our export trades down to a level enabling us to expand our overseas markets on the one hand, and on the other to hold a larger proportion of our own markets against foreign imports.

It seems, therefore, evident that we cannot go ahead in a high-wage policy for our sheltered occupations without regard to the possibly injurious reactions of this policy on the real wages in our lower-paid unsheltered occupations, and on our volume of overseas trade. Only so far as the high-wage policy in the former is a direct stimulation of other cost

economies at least adequate to compensate the higher
wage bill, is this wage policy economically justifiable.
If it does not so operate, it is a direct attack of the
economically stronger workers upon the weaker, and
renders more difficult any reduction of money wages
required to effect the export sales necessary to
purchase our overseas supplies.

In our shortsighted way we evade the issue by
stressing the two factors which at present enable us
to buy more foreign goods than we sell, viz. the
interest upon our overseas investments, and the
transport and other invisible exports. But the
shrinkage, not merely in the size and value, but in
the proportion of the world's trade which we hold,
and in the amount and value of our recent overseas
investments, make it unlikely that we can recover
our pre-war position, or even find the means to
pay for the increase of overseas goods needed to
maintain our population in the progressive standard
of living to which it has become accustomed. Every
effort to do this seems to involve a descent in the
standard of living for the export and other unsheltered trades towards the lower level of our
continental, and even possibly our new Asiatic
competitors. This painful process would bring out
into the open the cleavage of economic power and
the conflict of interests between sheltered and
exposed industries, a result which incidentally would
break the solidarity of labour in the trade union
movement and the labour party.

This is one more illustration of the irrationality and

injustice of an economic system where the distribution of the product is by a series of unequal pulls.

In the wider world economic system, given free mobility for capital and labour and goods, the problem above presented would be solved by a process of redistribution of economic resources based upon a recognition of the changes in the relative position of our country and its population as producers and consumers. It would be clearly recognised that this country had lost some of the relative advantages it had possessed in the past in manufactures, shipping, and finance, and that other countries could make a better use of some of the capital and labour which clung to our shores. The migration of this surplus labour and capital to other areas of the earth, where it could be more productively employed, would reduce *pro tanto* our dependence upon foreign trade, and our remaining population, probably further reduced by birth control, could continue living on a relatively high standard of comfort. Complete free trade, accompanied by some real international finance, would undoubtedly move a couple of millions or more of our superfluous workers into places where their work might be better utilised, and a corresponding amount of our investable capital might accompany them. The economic notion that our present population, with any increase we may choose to breed, can live on this island and produce by their work a real income that will give them a rising standard of comfort and leisure, is utterly quixotic. The quasi-rational support it receives from the immense recent advances in technological productivity only signifies that modern capitalism can with a given quantity of labour produce a greater quantity of goods. It does not signify that this economy can be adequately realised in a particular national area for an unlimited population.

There are, indeed, three conditions upon which our still growing population can be kept upon this national area. The one is that a large section of them will conform to the lower standard of consumption which prevails among their competitors in the world market. The second is that the surplus received in the form of profits and wages by the sheltered industries should be taken by taxation and used to subsidise the capital and labour of the unsheltered industries. This could be done honestly by direct taxation of the higher incomes in these latter, or by subsidies from the yield of a protective tariff, which would, however, reduce the general real income of the working classes.

If, as is likely, neither of these conditions is feasible or acceptable, the third course is to use the economic and political instruments of internationalism to raise the standard of life in the lower areas of the economic system. A rise of real wages towards our level in countries competing with us in the world market would exercise a double influence in easing our economic situation. It would reduce the serious handicap we suffer from 'sweated' labour operating up-to-date machinery and underselling us in Asiatic and other markets. But far more important, it would so stimulate consumption in these vast areas of low-paid labour, China, India, Russia, Africa, that the full productivity of modern industrialism could be employed in meeting the growing demand of the great populations in these backward lands.

Thus, and thus alone, can the virtually illimitable advance of productivity in the modern economic system be applied so as to provide for all the peoples that sufficiency of material commodities and of leisure which are now for the first time in the history of man economically available. These productive powers are at present held in leash by the failure of consumption to afford the necessary stimulus. The consumer for whose enjoyments the whole of this economic system is supposed to have been created is unable to perform his necessary part of with-drawing goods from the productive system as fast as they can be produced. This failure on his part is due to a distribution of money incomes that is unfavour-able to an adequate demand for commodities.

This disease has, we see, a definitely moral cause. It is due to attempts of individuals and groups to use economic force, chance, cunning, and opportunity, for selfish ends, and to construct and operate an economic system in accordance with this defective morale. The last and longest phase of this immorality is economic nationalism, by which organised financial, industrial, and trading groups within a nation strive to direct its political and economic policy so as to secure for themselves as large a share as possible of the world's wealth "under the name and pretext of the commonwealth." Thus a protectionist, imperialist, militarist system is maintained in order that these interests may make profits by isolating the home market and taxing "the consumer," by employing the diplomatic and, in the last resource, the armed force of their country to secure the possession of the natural resources and the labour of backward countries for their profitable exploitation. The incidental gain which such a policy may win for the nation to which these business interests adhere is sometimes real and is always envisaged as a contributory motive by business imperialists. The blend of competitive and co-operative imperialism which marks the modern controls of Western powers over Africa is the most conspicuous example of this sham economic nationalism. Sham, because the methods of acquisition and control, including the reaction of this imperialism upon the relations of competing Western powers, if expressed in a true balance sheet, would nearly always show a deficit which the taxpayer had to bear. But this aspect of economic nationalism and imperialism is not, as we recognise, its chief condemnation. There are two really damning counts in the charge against it. First, that by treating backward lands and populations as material for profitable exploitation it employs cheap and usually forced labour, so bringing into play that very sweating system which prevents the demand for consumable goods from keeping pace with the enlarged productivity of the Western world. It is a definite instrument for maldistribution of the world's income.

Secondly, it debases the moral currency by feeding the hypocrisy that covers gainful exploitation by the pretext of a civilising mission, concerned with the elevation of the native population, a "sacred trust." While many missionaries and some high-minded officials are really concerned with the welfare of the people, the business 'settlers' are concerned almost exclusively with such government as will enable them to get the largest gain in the shortest time out of native labour applied to natural resources under white supervision, and so enable them to quit the rôle of 'settler.'

The conflict of economic interests, which we have traced in the narrower spheres of the business, the industry, the national economy, is here seen in its most extensive application, partly as a conflict between national groups of business men using the title and power of their respective nations, but partly as an inter-imperialism by which the capitalist organisations of several countries in co-operation mark down backward countries for an economic exploitation which definitely worsens the distribution of the enlarged world-production, by converting large low-producing but self-sustaining populations into the low-paid tools of a higher productivity.

Summarising this process in its bearing upon the policy of high wages, we conclude that, while it may be gainful to a particular business, or a particular trade, or even a particular country, to pay such low wages as will enable it to undersell competitors, as a world policy it is suicidal. It is the supreme example of the separatist fallacy, the belief that what may be good for any must be good for all.

But though it is seen to be a literally vital interest of high-waged countries, like England and the United States, to secure an international policy which by raising the wages and consuming power in lower-waged countries shall bring about an expansion of world markets adequate to give full employment to their increasing powers of production, two difficulties confront them. First, there is the case of white Western countries, with long-established, low-wage standards, but whose technical equipment and organisation for export trade are as good as, or better than, those of England and America. It cannot any longer be argued that high wages are essential as a stimulus to mechanical improvements and other economies of overhead charges. Efficiency wages on a customary level suffice in continental countries, and labour organisations in these countries seem unable by collective bargaining to raise the wage-level near to ours or the American. Secondly, there is the rise of capitalist production in Asiatic and African countries employing cheap voluntary or forced native labour. Japan is, of course, the most conspicuous case, for its successful advance in the export trade of the East is definitely due to cheap labour operating modern manufacturing plants. In India, China, and parts of Africa a similar capitalism, with labour even cheaper than that of Japan, though less efficient in quality and control, is making considerable advances.

Both these groups of lower-waged countries may stand out against our proposed policy of high wages and better distribution as the means of securing full utilisation of the world's productive power. Their capitalists may see an easier and more immediately gainful policy in using the economy of cheap labour to get for themselves a larger share of the limited market, putting out of action more and more of the plant and labour of the high-waged countries. Indifferent to the wider problem of world-industry, they may be satisfied to pursue a successful economic nationalism. Our debts and reparation policy stimulates Germany and other debtor countries to adopt this policy, and China, India, and Russia may decide to make large gains out of foreign trade at the expense of smaller and less profitable home markets. This course is not advantageous to the peoples of these countries, but capitalism does not heed national advantages, and where public power is needed to further this policy it will endeavour to direct it.

There is, of course, a middle course which Western capitalism might choose. If trade unionism, in other countries as here, is able, either by the use of political machinery or by 'direct action,' to menace or to sabotage the more profitable forms of capitalism, there might occur a number of formal or informal deals between capital and labour which would give to the latter in wages, hours, and other conditions a satisfactory or sufficient share of the gains from the exploitation of the lower races. This inter-imperialism, or combined policy of Western capitalisms, might by raising the consuming power of the white peoples, so increase the demand for standardised commodities as to give a further lease of life to the capitalist system. The conflicts between capital and labour in the Western world might temporarily be healed by an extension of the rigours of capitalist exploitation in China, India, Africa, and Russia.[1] The expansion of markets for commodities in Western lands might for a time keep modern rationalised industry in full employment. But not for long. For this inter-capitalism must soon reach the end of its tether. The conflicts of economic interest, which we have been analysing, between capital and labour within the single business and industry, between sheltered and unsheltered industries within each nation, between Western national capitalisms, struggling for a restricted world market, will have now given place to a final conflict between the economic interests of the advanced and backward peoples. But as the productivity of Western capitalism continues to advance, probably with an accelerating pace as industry gets further aids from science, the problem of under-consumption, the failure of markets to expand fast enough, is bound to reassert itself. For this problem is rooted in the ethics of exploitation, the settlement of bargains or prices by economic force instead of by accepted principles of fair play or humanity. Recurrent world-depressions would continue to happen owing to the fact that the world's

[1] The present Soviet economic system is none the less 'capitalist' in method because the State assumes the rôle of capitalist.

income would be so wrongfully distributed that the demand for standardised goods could not keep pace with the enlarged capacity to turn out such goods.

The conscious ordering of world industry and commerce as the organic whole it is, can alone serve to give peace, prosperity, and progress to the economic life of the several parts of that organic whole. The simple fact that we are members one of another underlies all the complexities of trade relations, though it has never yet been apprehended and realised in terms of any central organic government. This indispensable condition of the safety and civilisation of the world is, indeed, very difficult to attain. For those primitive irrationalities and injustices, which we have seen incorporated in the ordinary processes of business and the minds of men, the notion that a man 'makes his income,' that the ordinary operations of a market give each buyer and seller 'his due,' and that the competitive system tends to give each man 'what he is worth'—these follies and falsehoods are difficult to uproot from the minds of those who think their private interests menaced by the process.

But those who hold that this capitalism can only be destroyed by force and that the peoples are or can be possessed of the necessary force are doubly in error. For, in the first place, there is little reason to believe that the organisation of working peoples is anywhere possessed of the force required for a successful proletarian revolution. Recent events in Russia are the strongest corroboration of this view.

By common admission the present government,
political and economic, of that country is a self-
appointed oligarchy employing the extreme methods
of capitalist control, during a period of alleged transi-
tion to a democratic socialism rendered ever more
difficult by the permeation of arbitrary force throughout the veins of industry.

But if capitalism could be overthrown by popular
force, there is no reason to believe that this mode
of overthrow would help the intricate task of re-
organising the economic system on an equitable
basis. On the contrary, formally successful revolutionary force would leave the workers' minds poisoned
and disabled for performance of their task. Effective
government in any branch of conduct requires the
real consent not merely of a triumphant majority, but
of the defeated minority. The root errors, moral and
intellectual, which have sustained the hitherto dominant minority in their dominance, must be exposed to
their holders. In other words, the moral force rightly
at the disposal of the proletariat is a much more
potent instrument for economic reform than the
physical force which they erroneously believe that
they possess. For the new economic revolution should
be a process not of destruction followed by construc-
tion, but of adaptation and displacement, with a
clear consciousness of the moral and intellectual
nature of this process. I do not assert that rational
reform can wholly dispense with physical compulsion.
But its success will require that a substantial number
of the 'capitalist class' are won over by the appeal to

justice and humanity and recognise the need for conscious economic government. It may be necessary to coerce a refractory minority of the minority, whose will is obdurate against appeals to equity or reason. This belongs to the tragedy of all great reformations. But the general cause of conscious economic world-government is of such plain and poignant appeal to the common sense and decent feeling of all sorts and conditions of men that it would be a calamity to weaken its legitimate force by recourse to those weapons of coercion and ill will that have been responsible for those very evils we are seeking to cure.

One comment upon the current internationalism represented by the various institutions of the League of Nations and other organisations for the handling of world problems is necessary here. The progress of a genuinely international government, whether for economic or for other human purposes, does not consist merely, or mainly, in improved arrangements for enabling national governments, or national economic groups, to pursue their national aims without conflict, or even with some limited measure of co-operation. Though, for many economic, political, cultural, and other purposes, nations are likely to retain separate national governments, the ambit of those interests and activities that affect the general well-being of mankind will continually increase. Now this general well-being is something quite different from the addition of the well-being of the several national units, and its government is not achieved by institutions which national representatives strive to utilise for their respective national interests. This supremely important and essentially moral issue stands out very clearly in the initial and experimental life of the Geneva institutions. National self-sufficiency and national interests are predominant in most of its so-styled internationalism. The task is to resolve initial oppositions of interest into some moderate harmony by a process of mutual concessions. This, however, is a wasteful process. Not until the moral, political, and economic harmony of mankind becomes the normal initial and fundamental assumption of all its activities is the basis of co-operative internationalism truly laid. In other words, the displacement of national by human sentiment, involving a willingness sometimes to sacrifice the interests of one's own nation for the general good of humanity, is the spirit needed to make the mind of modern man conform to the moral and economic fabric of the world in which we live.

CHAPTER VI

A MORAL REFORMATION

A brief summary of my argument may here be given. My thesis is that our main economic troubles are of a distinctively moral origin. An element of inequitable force, penetrating all the marketing arrangements by which wealth is distributed among those who, by personal activity or possessions, contribute to the productive processes, is seen to paralyse productivity, causing unemployment and waste of all the productive powers of nature and of men. This inequitable force distributes income neither in accordance with personal costs, nor efforts, nor needs, but in proportion to unequal pulls, whose strength depends upon the natural or contrived scarcity of some factor of production in some market. Such economic force has a double effect in maldistribution. It not only enables the stronger individual or group to get the better of the weaker and rob the latter of its proper share, but it enables the stronger to rob society of the social contribution which co-operates with each individual or group in making values. Thus the workers as a whole are wronged by the economic forces which accord too large a share of the product to non-workers. Sheltered workers by their superior force in bargaining injure unsheltered workers. Owners of natural resources are able to extort large payments for which they perform no services. These payments are extracted in part from the incomes of those who do perform productive services. Thus in the distribution of private incomes there takes place a double waste, some members of the community getting more than is required to evoke and sustain the services they render, others getting less.

But an even graver injury is wrought by ignoring the part which the whole economic system plays in giving social value to each particular product. While the most individualistic business man will agree that 'market conditions' determine the price he will get for anything he sells, he rarely stops to consider what the term 'market conditions' means. He fails to see that it covers the business activities of the innumerable other men who contribute to the supply of the goods he sells, and to the demand for those goods. Still less does he see that the 'demand' in a market brings in, as direct determinants of the value of his goods, the entire body of other men who form the human factor in the economic world system. If he could be got to realise these truths, he might adopt a different attitude towards taxation, recognising it as a legitimate attempt of the State, as representative of economic society, to claim back from individual recipients of income some part of the income due to society in virtue of its productive efforts. He might be led on to recognise that, just as he needs some income, in order that he may do his work properly and help to develop and enjoy a full personality, so does society. He might then see the development of social services, or communal life, not as a movement hostile to private property and private enterprise, but as a supplementary and serviceable element. A strong, healthy personality can only thrive in a strong, healthy community. The latter requires its due share of the income it helps to make. There is no rigid fixed limit to that share. As in the case of the individual so in that of the community, capacity to put to a good use is the true test.

Our argument has shown how by correcting the inequities of distribution under current capitalism the stoppages and wastes which mar its present operations can be avoided. We have seen that while no adequate remedies can be found within the area of economic nationalism, alleviations may be applied within the narrower circle.

One final misconception that may arise I desire here to remove. The exposure of the moral defects of current capitalism may induce some readers to believe that some other single system, whether communism or State socialism, can and should be substituted. That conscious central planning should be put into the economic system is, I think, unquestionably true. But in that planning the most critical issue will be that of the proper moral relation between the individual and society, or, as I would prefer to put it, between personality and community. This is the problem of relating adequate economic incentives to economic needs. A slick all-round communism that would narrowly ration on an equalitarian basis the private incomes of all its members, and prescribe their methods of consumption, reserving the residue

for communal uses, though it might avoid some of
the sorts of waste disclosed by our present capitalism,
would certainly engender wastes of its own. Even if
the predominantly public services could be efficiently
administered, the virtual exclusion of the element of
private enterprise or adventure would be seriously
detrimental to progress in the arts of production.
Though some of the key and standard industries,
where free competition is either absent or detrimental,
must necessarily pass under public ownership and
control, while many 'social services' not directly
engaged in supplying 'economic needs' will absorb an
increasing proportion of the general income, two free
fields for private adventure are indispensable. One is
that of invention and experiment in new processes
and new commodities, where motives of gain or glory
and joy of discovery are inextricably blended. The
history of British industry is replete with examples
of this sort of individualistic activity which will continue to thrive, and for which freedom and adequate
incentives should be provided in our new economic
society. The other field of private enterprise lies in
the discovery and development of resources in backward countries where the conditions of work and life
cannot immediately be brought under the same
regimen as prevails in the more civilised parts of the
world. While the equitable treatment of labour and
the policy of raising wages in such countries form an
indispensable condition of world progress, and a due
share of the product must be applied through taxation to 'social services,' a large part of the direct

control of business operations will almost necessarily remain in the hands of private business undertakers. The mandatory system is the first stage in the supersession of national imperialism by a genuinely international government in this work of development.

Apart from these two fields of private enterprise, the new economic government, in displacing profiteering by public service, will not be able to apply indiscriminately either the absolute equalitarianism which Bernard Shaw has advocated or the strict principle of distribution according to needs. Wide personal divergences in productive capacity, especially in the higher qualities of intellectual work, will continue to enable their owners to extort rents of ability from society, to which they have no moral right, but which society must pay in order to get the best fruits of such ability. How far monetary payments can be displaced by other honourable distinctions is a not unimportant question of economic psychology. It may be expected that the general displacement of selfish force as the determinant of income by the concept of public utility, taken in conjunction with the larger supply of each order of ability from equality of educational and other opportunities, will greatly diminish the scarcity value of personal ability. Moreover, when the owner of some rare ability, industrial, artistic, or other, finds himself confronted no longer with the demand of rich private competing bidders, but with a single public buyer, or, in the case of an artist, singer, player, with a public of moderately incomed buyers, the rent of his ability inevitably falls. But so long as, and so far as, a man of ability is bent on selfish gain, it will be necessary for society to let him have as much as is requisite to get the use of his ability.

The policy of distribution according to needs must take into account the selfish element in the psychology of incentives. But experience of public service, not only in the fighting departments but in the civil, shows how small is the part played by differentiation of income in evoking and sustaining skilled personal activities. With the displacement of profiteering from the general body of industry, it is reasonable to expect that lavish expenditure will cease to be regarded as the chief criterion of a successful career, and that the craving for personal prestige will find other more honourable modes of expression. But idealists would do well to reflect upon the certainty that in the best reformed society elements of selfish recalcitrance will remain, and that scope must be found for the arts of concession and compromise. The very banality of such copybook maxims testifies to the persistence of the truth which they embody.

These qualifications, however, are not calculated seriously to impair the principle of equitable distribution as a reliable instrument for utilising modern powers of production so as to secure a reasonable standard of life for mankind.

INDEX

For Product Safety Concerns and Information please contact our EU
representative GPSR@taylorandfrancis.com Taylor & Francis Verlag GmbH,
Kaufingerstraße 24, 80331 München, Germany

Printed and bound by CPI Group (UK) Ltd, Croydon, CR0 4YY
08/05/2025
01864362-0001